E♭ Alto Saxophone

Audio Access Included

Great Carols

Instrumental Solos for Christmas   Selected by James Curnow

Contents

PLAYBACK+
Speed • Pitch • Balance • Loop

To access audio, visit:
www.halleonard.com/mylibrary
Enter Code
2793-4405-1935-2337

ISBN 978-90-431-1890-3

CURNOW MUSIC

EXCLUSIVELY DISTRIBUTED BY

HAL•LEONARD®

Visit Hal Leonard Online at
www.halleonard.com

World headquarters, contact:
Hal Leonard
7777 West Bluemound Road
Milwaukee, WI 53213
Email: info@halleonard.com

In Europe, contact:
Hal Leonard Europe Limited
1 Red Place
London, W1K 6PL
Email: info@halleonardeurope.com

In Australia, contact:
Hal Leonard Australia Pty. Ltd.
4 Lentara Court
Cheltenham, Victoria, 3192 Australia
Email: info@halleonard.com.au

INTRODUCTION

This collection of some of the world's greatest Christmas carols was created for, and is dedicated to, Philip Smith, Principal Trumpet, New York Philharmonic Orchestra. The goal of these arrangements is to allow instrumentalists the opportunity to give praise and adoration to God through their musical abilities.

Though these arrangements were written specifically with Phil in mind, attention has been given to the needs of all of the individual instruments. Through the use of cued notes, players of differing ability levels will be able to perform these arrangements.

Each solo book includes online audio which includes both a sample performance of each solo, as well as the accompaniment only. This will allow the performer to practice with the accompaniment when an accompanist is not available. The accompaniment track can also be used for performances if desired. Appropriate tuning notes have been included to allow the soloist the opportunity to adjust their intonation to the intonation of the online audio accompaniment. A separate piano accompaniment book is available.

May you enjoy using this collection and find it useful in extending your musical ministry.

Kindest regards,

James Curnow
President
Curnow Music Press, Inc.

Great Carols
E♭ Alto Saxophone

Arranged by:
Stephen Bulla
Douglas Court
James Curnow
William Himes
Timothy Johnson
Kevin Norbury

ISBN 978-90-431-1890-3
Audio performed by Becky Shaw - Piano, Michael Rintamaa - Organ,
Recorded at Central Christian Church, Lexington, KY USA

1. JOY TO THE WORLD

Arr. **James Curnow** (ASCAP)

2. GOOD CHRISTIAN MEN, REJOICE

Arr. **Douglas Court** (ASCAP)

3. WHAT CHILD IS THIS?

Arr. **Stephen Bulla** (ASCAP)

Copyright © 2003 by **Curnow Music Press, Inc.**

4. O COME, ALL YE FAITHFUL

Based on an arrangement by Arlene Johnson

Arr. **Timothy Johnson** (ASCAP)

Copyright © 2003 by Curnow Music Press, Inc.

5. DING DONG MERRILY ON HIGH

Arr. **Kevin Norbury** (ASCAP)

6. IT CAME UPON THE MIDNIGHT CLEAR

Arr. **William Himes** (ASCAP)

7. ANGELS WE HAVE HEARD ON HIGH

Arr. **Stephen Bulla** (ASCAP)

Copyright © 2003 by **Curnow Music Press, Inc.**

8. O COME, O COME EMMANUEL

Arr. **Timothy Johnson** (ASCAP)

✳ *Optional repeat for live performance*
to measure 7

Copyright © 2003 by **Curnow Music Press, Inc.**

9. O LITTLE TOWN OF BETHLEHEM

Arr. **Douglas Court** (ASCAP)

Eb Alto Saxophone

13

10. HE IS BORN

Arr. **James Curnow** (ASCAP)

E♭ Alto Saxophone